Remodel
Green

Make Your House Serve Your Life

Book and cover design by the author

All photographs from the collection of Kelly and Rosana Hart,
except the photo of the windcatchers on page 21 is by Mostafa Aref Haghi
Paperback ISBN: 0-916289-38-9

Printed in the United States of America

First printing June, 2014

Hartworks, Inc.
P. O. Box 632
Crestone, CO 81131

Email: theoffice@hartworks.com

Websites: www.hartworks.com
www.greenhomebuilding.com
www.dreamgreenhomes.com

Table of Contents

Foreword

We're facing some pretty big questions today: for example, how long can we continue consuming over 1.5 times Earth's available resources and survive? And knowing this, how can we continue to employ existing growth-based economic, political and behavioral models that ever expand our population, power, resource-utilization and earthly dominion?

Energy-usage is the crux of this global-growth-paradigm-problem. Continued expansion in fossil-fuel energy systems brought global carbon emissions to nearly 36 billion metric tons in 2013 (up 2.1% from 2012). We've also passed 400.0 parts per million (ppm) in the atmosphere, far above the 350 ppm consensus target, and over 60% above the 1997 Kyoto Protocol's baseline levels. A recent IPCC (International Panel on Climate Change) report shows that climate change is human-exacerbated, impacting all areas of the planet with more intense weather, greater floods, droughts, more severe storms, etc.

The obvious yet still-elusive answer to these problems involves bringing our ravenous human appetites under control. We need a more balanced, integral relationship with nature, perhaps even the possibility of reducing our consumption enough to promote the healthy regeneration of critical natural systems. Unfortunately, such a "steady-state" or even shrinking form of collective behavioral footprint hasn't yet replaced our de facto global growth model, whose tentacles have claimed all facets of our lives. So our expanding global consumption has birthed an era of ever more extreme climate challenge.

To survive and thrive, our hard-won freedoms and rights (such as the freedom to pollute or grow without restriction) must be tempered with an even greater responsibility for Earth's intricate web of life and the living systems that unceasingly support us.

The "reduce, re-use, recycle" green mantra has thus become a critically important, action-based change-driver to this end. Use of alternative energy systems, re-use of existing structures (whose associated carbon footprint is a fait accompli with minimal climate impact), moving beyond fossil fuels, thus lowering our carbon emissions further, have all become global imperatives. Such reduction efforts are simply the most intelligent, life-saving, crucial activities we can undertake today.

Enter one Kelly Hart, a dear old friend and long-time collaborator in the sustainability movement. In this field of endeavor, Kelly is equal parts bricoleur, inventor, climate champion and genius. He has dedicated his entire adult life to this arena, working in admirable ways that are "low-tech," compassion-based, and achievable by all.

Remodel Green is a new volume in his recent Green Building series. It furthers his signature hands-on, down-to-earth, grass-roots, DIY approach. Like the earlier *Rolling Shelter*, we can rely here primarily on Kelly's own experience – his expansive, pertinent knowledge that is well-conceived, written and organized, and richly illustrated with his own photos throughout.

This volume focuses specifically on remodeling existing structures with energy-efficiency in mind – an important and relevant yet often-overlooked sustainability model. It provides multiple avenues and benefits for reducing energy and resource consumption: For example, the re-use of existing structures significantly reduces associated construction-related emissions (since the structures already exist). The energy-efficiency remodeling focus also greatly reduces the structure's operating carbon footprint. These two aspects provide synergistic benefits for the environment.

As always, Kelly's presentation proceeds clearly and sequentially as we investigate the stages of various projects from early planning to final product. His genuine love of the renovation and efficiency-increasing design process – always uniting with it directly and innovatively – and the ingenuity he brings to bear on every aspect of these interesting remodeling efforts, is impressive and inspiring.

Each chapter begins with important general principles subsequently illustrated with concrete experiential examples from Kelly's extensive multi-decade career. Fundamental green and sustainability-based elements and principles are featured throughout. Such "typical" sustainability-oriented remodeling situations include: Passive solar design and the use of thermal mass for heating and cooling, photo-voltaic home power systems, natural/recycled materials, home gardening, food storage, rainwater catchment and more.

What is not typical is Kelly's great love, mastery and wisdom fleshing out the how's and why's in these life situations. He shares not only the relevant systems rationale, but also the value they each hold – why it's important to employ them whenever possible. This teaches us how to think sustainably for ourselves.

He believes, as many of us do, that it all comes down to reducing fossil-fuel energy usage and enhancing life quality in the process. As Kelly says, it's all about "how best to utilize existing resources to make our future more pleasant."

This simple, step-by-step healing magic perfectly counters the ultimate challenge of our time. Kelly demonstrates convincingly that this humble approach can move us out of the danger zone and into a trajectory toward a safe, vibrant future. He shows us how our global climate crisis can be turned into delight -- right here, right now, where we each live our lives. Thank you Kelly for bringing us just what the doctor ordered! Hallelujah!

Lee Temple, PrimaMundi.com

Introduction

There are many reasons for remodeling. It could be the desire for greater comfort in your home from improved insulation or heating and cooling options. Or perhaps you want to create new space for activities or family members. Or maybe you hope to achieve increased efficiency and savings on utility bills. Sometimes toxic materials can be replaced with more benign, natural choices. Perhaps you want your house to be more attractive. All of these goals can be accomplished with a carefully planned remodel.

To renovate a home is one of the ultimate ways of recycling, taking an existing structure and using it as a basis for creating just what you need. This is certainly a more sustainable choice than building an entirely new home that would likely entail the use of much more material with all of its embodied energy and negative ecological impact.

Whether you plan to remodel an existing house or build a new one, the principles for doing so in a sustainable, green way are the same. Each chapter in this book will explore one the fundamental tenets of building green.

Over the course of my life I have engaged in numerous remodelling projects, as a professional carpenter, as a home owner, and as a renter. I'll be drawing on this experience as I explore with you what I consider to be the main principles that should guide you in your choices for your own green remodelling project.

Fitting Your House to Your Needs

Life is a fluid affair. Circumstances are always changing. Families enlarge and contract; employment and interests change. Making your house accommodate these changes as they occur will make your life flow much better.

From a more basic perspective, we have biological needs that we expect our house to serve. We want to be comfortable, neither too hot nor too cold. We want to have hot and cold water available. We want the electricity we need to run appliances, lights, etc. We want clean air to breathe. And we want all of this be provided without harming us or the environment.

The first step in planning to remodel your house is a realistic needs assessment. What aspects of your life are not being served adequately by your current home? How could you change things to bring your house more into alignment with your needs?

One approach to evaluating your needs is to make a list of all the various activities that you can imagine doing regularly in your house. You might do this as a brainstorming session with your spouse or children, without immediately judging the relevance of each idea. Then once you have your list you can go back and note how important each function is and to what extent your current situation satisfies it. This process should result in a list of activities that your house is not currently serving well and help you evaluate what sorts of remodeling options might contribute to greater well being and satisfaction.

While you are evaluating your list, bear in mind that living modestly and compactly are virtues in terms of green living. This is true from several standpoints. Smaller spaces both require less materials to build and less energy to keep comfortable. This likely means less expense and less house work. And there is often the added convenience of having possessions near at hand.

You may have noticed the popularity of tiny houses these days. People are discovering that they can be happy in much less space. I can attest to this through my experience living in a variety of vehicle-based homes, from buses to vans, as detailed in my first book in this series, *Rolling Shelter: Vehicles We Have Called Home.*

As an example of this principle, several years ago my wife, Rosana, and I bought an inexpensive used manufactured home to use as a basis for developing a small ecological homestead. This house had a footprint of about 1100 square feet, with two bedrooms. We both work at home and we each really need our own office, so one of the bedrooms would become an office... but where would the second office be? We made a drawing of the existing floor plan and made little cutouts of our furniture. It took several days to settle on a plan that suited both of us, but we were determined to make it work without immediately enlarging the house.

In this photo you can see what the living room was like when we bought the house. There was a wood stove in the corner of the L-shaped living room, and a hall going back to the rest of the house on the right. We determined that the only practical candidate for carving out a second office was the area where the stove and its brick surround was located. So we embarked on a project to remove the stove and the brick arrangement. This left a hole in the ceiling where the stove pipe had been, which we converted to a light well. The hole in the wall where there had been an air inlet for the stove became a cat door to a cat enclosure just outside the wall.

This photo, taken from roughly the same angle as the previous one, shows how we extended the hallway with two large bookcases at right angles to each other. There was a space between them for doorway access to the new office nook. At first we thought that this would be a temporary solution and that eventually we would enlarge the house to accommodate a separate office. Now we have become accustomed to this arrangement and prefer the convenience that it provides in its proximity to all of the other functions of the house. Obviously the living room is smaller, about half the size it used to be, but it is big enough to suit the way we use it.

We had similar challenges in two other houses we have owned. One of these was in Mexico where we had bought a tiny two-room cabin. There we simply partitioned a portion of the bedroom space for an office.

In Olympia, Washington, we converted a garage to serve several functions, including an office. The photo shows Rosana and me not long after we bought this little house. The garage in question is on the

right. A contractor had completely refurbished this house with new plumbing, wiring, windows, etc. before we bought it.

In order to make the office comfortable and thermally efficient, I fitted panels of 3-inch rigid insulation between all of the wall studs and the spaces between the rafter ties that framed the ceiling. You can see how those rafter ties were also supported by a couple of major beams so that it was safe to walk into the attic area above.

The walls were simply covered with gypsum board and painted.

The attic storage space we created above the ceiling was accessible from the second story of this small house. So what had been a rather standard, uninsulated garage attached to the house was divided into a large office, a small shop, and attic storage space. Our plan was to build another actual garage behind the house, which we eventually did.

The other side of the office space in that garage became a small shop and storage area, with the original garage door opening into it.

Outside of the old garage I dug down low enough around the perimeter of the foundation to insert 2-inch rigid blueboard insulation below the level of the poured concrete floor pad. This helped keep that thermal mass from bleeding warmth into the ground. I placed aluminum flashing under the outside sheathing and fitted it over the rigid blueboard to protect what was exposed above grade after the area was backfilled, and to keep rain from working its way between the concrete and the insulation.

Why did I used industrial insulation products in this remodel? The answer is that there really are no naturally available materials with the same characteristics. The blueboard insulation is water impermeable and can be placed below grade without degradation; the foam board used on the inside provides considerably more insulation value than an equivalent thickness of something like wool or denim insulation would. I think that the overall enhanced thermal efficiency of using these products easily offset the energy used in manufacturing and transporting them to my site.

Another experimental aspect of this garage remodel was to make a kind of thermal mass heater using the existing natural gas domestic water heater as the heat source. Along the outside foundation wall that was exposed on the inside of the office, I made a loop of half inch copper pipe embedded between ceramic tiles fixed to the concrete foundation wall below the desk. In the photo, if you look just above the floor, you can see where that loop was since the grout that covered it is darker than the rest of the area.

This water circuit was plumbed directly to the hot water outlet of the water heater in such a way that I could turn some valves and force the hot water to flow through the mass and return to the cold inlet line of the water heater, thus heating that mass. I installed an ordinary hot water circulating pump that is used to keep hot water easily accessible at faucets a long distance from the water heater. So with the turn of a couple of valves and a switch to turn on the pump, I could heat my office. This system worked pretty well.

After I did the installation, I discovered that it is not a good idea to embed copper pipe in concrete because it can corrode. These days, I would choose common pex tubing for this job.

A mistake that I made in converting the unheated garage to heated space didn't surface until several years later when we wanted to sell the house. A potential buyer ordered a home inspection which revealed that the roof of the attic over the garage was rotting and the OSB sheathing of the roof was turning to mush. Why? Because I neglected to provide adequate ventilation for the attic. This wasn't necessary with the original garage since it was not heated and condensation forming on the inside was unlikely. But with a heated space, the warm moist air rose into the attic and condensed on the cold surfaces of the roof.

The way to avoid this is to put soffit vents under the eaves of the roof and ridge vents at the peak of the roof. I had to pay to have this done in order to sell the house. This was a substantial job because the roof had to be completely removed and new sheathing and then shingles put on. Sometimes we learn lessons the hard way!

Sunshine Camp is another example of creating a home from an existing structure. Actually, in this case, it was a whole row of five little cabins joined together by a walkway and another one nearby at a lower level. These had been sleeping cabins at an old Catholic children's summer camp that we bought in the mid 1970's with two of my sisters and their families. I will write more about the communal life later, but at this point I want to explain how we made a home out of this odd arrangement.

These cabins were pretty funky, with rotting pier foundations and no insulation. Fortunately somebody had put metal roofs over them, so at least they weren't leaking.

One cabin was a little larger than the others, and it became our immediate abode. The walls of this one had been insulated and paneled, so it was more comfortable generally. It had a minimal kitchen and enough space to have a dining table and a sofa.

The first order of business in restoring our cabins was to arrest the rotting of the foundations by raising them further off the ground and installing permanent concrete piers and new wooden support posts. Once that was done we were able to put our attention to creating our own bathroom.

The photo on the next page shows how we made a deck between our bedroom cabin on the left and my office on the right. This was roofed over to shed water down a common gutter. Near our dog were the studs framing the new bathroom next to the bedroom. A doorway was cut between the two for easy access. Since the bedroom and my office were on different levels we created a series of terraced steps or planter ledges running the length of the space between the two cabins.

Besides the living/dining/kitchen cabin, we designated other functions to each of the other five cabins. One became our bedroom, another my office/studio, one for storage, one for Rosana's office/pottery studio, and the last was guest space, especially for when my daughter was visiting.

You may have noticed that this doesn't account for a bathroom. Not far from our row of cabins was the communal bathing and toilet facility which we used until we were able to create our personal bathroom adjacent to our bedroom.

The redwood lap siding was salvaged and many of the windows were odd pieces of stained glass left over from some of my sister's stained glass work.

We were very pleased to have our own bathroom.

I will describe the toilet in a subsequent chapter about water conservation, since it was a compost toilet.

Had we stayed longer than the seven years we were at Sunshine Camp, we probably would have combined the row of cabins into a single larger structure. I had drawings of how this might look. But for the time we were there, those cabins served our needs very well.

Invite the Sun into Your Home

I am a strong proponent of solar heating and have employed this concept in many of my remodeling projects. It makes so much sense from every aspect of sustainable architecture to use solar energy to heat your home, whether it is active or passive (with or without pumps and fans). Unless you live in one of those tropical climates that seldom needs additional heat to be comfortable, then I urge you to invite the sun into your home as a warming guest.

I am partial to passive solar concepts, mainly because they are simple and direct, with few moving parts to install and maintain. Really, it is a matter of basic architectural planning to devise an effective passive solar scheme. You need south-facing windows (in the Northern Hemisphere). You need some thermal mass inside to soak up the heat (preferably in direct contact with the sunshine). You need a well insulated envelope around the exterior skin of your home. And you need some way to insulate the windows at night to help keep the heat inside. Well designed roof eaves or other shading devices can help keep the sunshine from entering during the summer when the additional heat is not welcome.

There is a science to calculating exactly how much south-facing window area is needed to heat a given sized room, and how much thermal mass should be installed to store the heat. In doing the math you also need to factor in your climate and location relative to the angle of the sun on the solstices. It can get fairly complex, and I encourage anyone who wants to go about the design in a scientific manner to find a good book devoted to passive solar architecture; there are several of them listed on the *Resources* page.

In Edward Mazria's *The Passive Solar Energy Book*, he advocates that "In cold climates (average winter temperatures 20 to 30 degrees F.) provide between 0.19 and 0.38 square feet of south-facing glass for each square foot of space floor area. In temperate climates (average winter temperatures 35 to 45 degrees F.) provide 0.11 to 0.25 square feet of south-facing glass for each square foot of space floor area. This amount of glazing will admit enough sunlight to keep the space at an average of 65 to 70 degrees F. during much of the winter."

In my own remodeling to include passive solar concepts I have tended to a more seat-of-the-pants approach, and this has generally worked out well... perhaps because I have had a lot of experience doing this.

The orientation of the passive solar windows does not have to be perfectly facing south. The building can be up to 15 degrees either east or west of south and still perform well. In fact, where I am living now, high in the Colorado mountains, I added an extra east-facing window to capture more of the morning sun in the winter, and it is very welcome. During the summer I use venetian blinds to block the sunlight from those windows.

In general, though, it is best to minimize windows that face other directions than south, especially to the north and west. North windows are always going to be a net loss of heat and west windows tend to be hard to shade for afternoon sun and thus bring in too much heat during the summer.

A house that we owned in Ashland, Oregon lacked any significant southern windows, so we decided to add a separate sun space on the south side of the house. The idea was to use this space to help heat the home, as well as provide a pleasant place to grow some plants and have a hot tub for relaxing. In fact we even got a tax credit from the state of Oregon for adding this renewable energy device.

The concrete floor pad and foundation wall for the windows were insulated with foam insulation boards to isolate that thermal mass. Then the floor was covered with decorative tiles. This was the primary mass for storing heat in the space, but we had to be careful to not absorb too much of that heat in the room itself because the idea was to pass it on to the rest of the house. (Oregon actually had software to analyze this to determine if we were eligible for the tax credit.)

We cut a door into our living room from the sun room which we would open during the day to let in the heat. There was an openable window into our bedroom that would do the same, and another door into the utility room.

The roof over the sun space had a sufficient overhang to eliminate most of the summer sun, but we also added some shades on the outside of the glass that we could roll down if needed. We would often eat meals in that lovely space, as it also looked out onto our rose garden.

Another example of creating a sun space to help heat a home was actually a rental in Bernal, Mexico. Rosana and I wanted to spend more time in Mexico and found this cheap (about $100 US/month) rental that suited our needs. What it looked like when we first found it is shown below. It was very rustic in a typical Mexican way... all created with concrete blocks and poured concrete. The entry door fronted right on the sidewalk outside, and then there was a room just off the entry that became our bedroom. A minimal kitchen and bathroom were housed in the space under the balcony where Rosana is standing. The two upstairs rooms we intended to use as separate offices. This arrangement lacked any real living or dining space that was under roof.

We realized that it would be possible to put a roof over the concrete and tiled open courtyard, and make the whole house much more functional for our uses. We asked the landlord, who lived next door, if he would be amenable to this and he agreed to let us do it. After all, it would clearly increase the value of his property.

So we embarked on this project over the course of a few weeks, spending some of our own money to make it happen. To bridge the space between the walls of the courtyard I used tubular steel with a rectangular cross section. This is commonly available and less expensive than wood, which is hard to come by in Mexico. I arranged a slight pitch to the roof to shed water to the ground in the back yard. Over the metal supports I attached translucent corrugated fiberglass roofing panels. Our idea was that we could cover and uncover the roof seasonally with palm fronds to either shade the room below or allow the sun in for heat.

You can see how I worked on the project by attaching one row of panels at a time, placing the palm fronds on as I proceeded.

Obviously there is no insulation used in any of the materials in the house, so the concept wouldn't work out too well in many climates. That area of Mexico is rather temperate, but cool enough in the winter months that the extra heat would be welcome.

Below is a view of what it looked like in the end. The walls were painted with pigmented limewash very inexpensively. The window and door frame arrangement happened to be in the landlord's shed and he offered it to use for the remodel. This was ideal for the purpose, with openable window vents at the top and one sliding window panel to allow ventilation. All I had to do after securing the metal frame was hire a local glass shop to install the glass.

The laundry alcove beneath the stairs going up to the balcony was typical for Mexico where most laundry is done by hand.

This is what the interior space was like with the palm fronds in place and a heavy fabric curtain pulled across the glass front. This simple remodel made a huge difference in comfort and practicality of the house.

Once again we decided to take on a remodeling project to enclose the veranda as a sun space. This both helped heat the house and provided another interior room as a true living and dining room. This was fairly easy to do because the roof was already there and the bricked support pillars could be used to attach sliding glass doors that we had manufactured to precisely fit those spaces. The floor had been nicely tiled before we bought the house.

By an odd twist of fate, soon after we finished remodeling that rental, Rosana and I fell in love with a piece of property in the Lake Chapala region of Mexico which we managed to buy. This large lot had been landscaped extensively with trees and ornamentals, and included a swimming pool and a tiny cabin.

The house was basically a two-room cabin with a large covered veranda in the front. We managed to divide the larger of the two rooms into areas that served as both office and bedroom spaces. Much of the year it was possible to sit comfortably on the veranda, but we discovered that the entire house tended to be a bit cold during the winter months. After all, the walls were constructed of uninsulated bricks.

I bricked up the end walls, leaving openings for arched windows that could be opened for a cross breeze. Next to the existing windows into the house I opened up a skylight to allow sunlight in.

In order to make the sun space more thermally efficient I took the trouble to insulate the roof. I did this by filling polypropylene bags with crushed volcanic stone and suspending them in the voids between the roof rafters. I knew that this would work well since I had previously built an entire earthbag house with

15

a similar technique. The lightweight volcanic stone has many trapped air spaces that serve to insulate. To hold the bags in place, I stapled heavy duty wire mesh. Then, as a decorative ceiling, I attached inexpensive reed mats which covered the wire mesh and the bags. It made a noticeable difference in the comfort of that room once this ceiling treatment was complete.

The above photo shows the finished project from the outside. The amount of roof overhang was just about perfect for that climate and location.

The solar thermal panels on the roof beyond the sunroom were connected to the filtering system of the swimming pool and kept the pool comfortable for swimming much of the year.

After living in Mexico for five years we realized that we were missing our old community back in the mountains of Colorado. So we sold the Mexican property and set up residence in the manufactured home in Colorado mentioned earlier. The former owner had the foresight to orient the home with the long axis east-west, providing more opportunities for passive solar heat. In fact, she had already added on a passive solar greenhouse at one end of the south side.

There was not much of an eave to shade those windows during the summer, however. With the greenhouse, on the other hand, there was a substantial eave to help keep it cooler during the summer. When I put a new metal roof on the house, I extended the eave somewhat, but we still need to use our interior shades sometimes to avoid too much heat. At over 8,000 feet of elevation, the heating season is most of the year, so the extra heat in the spring and fall is generally welcome.

The home came with two rather large windows, side by side, on the south wall. Next to those two windows was enough space to put in another window to increase the solar heat gain, so that is what I did.

As I mentioned earlier, I also added an extra window facing the east. Not only does this bring in more morning sun, but also gives a more extensive view of the magnificent mountain range in that direction.

Along with windows that bring in the sun, any good passive solar design needs to employ plenty of thermal mass within the house interior. Thermal mass materials are dense and heavy, like stone, brick or tile. In this case, I installed about a ton of tile with its cement backing board over most of the floors of the entire house. We chose a dark tile that is better at absorbing heat than a lighter tile would be.

Behind the wood stove, I added another substantial heat sink by mortaring some of our lovely local rocks into a decorative heap. This easily adds another ton of thermal mass to the house, and helps hold the heat generated by the wood stove. All of this mass helps maintain a more stable temperature in the house during the cold season and also in the warm season.

All of the windows in the house have thermal shades that can be lowered. These are accordion-pleated shades made with an air space between the two membranes. They do let in some light when drawn during the day. In other houses I have used solid panels that provide more insulation, but these have to be stored somewhere when not in use.

In the greenhouse I made some rolling thermal shades from a kind of bubble wrap material faced on both sides with aluminized mylar to reflect radiant heat. The shades are fixed to a core of lightweight 4-inch PVC pipe that rolls up and down by pulling on two cords threaded through pulleys at the top. I have used this simple arrangement numerous times to create rolling shades for many applications. During the cold season, I lower these shades as soon as the sun goes down, and then raise them again in the morning.

Ways to Keep Your Cool

Keeping your house cool during hot weather can be challenging. The conventional approach of running an air conditioner is not a green solution; they are very energy intensive, often noisy, and don't provide uniformly comfortable indoor conditions.

Many of the same concepts employed for good passive solar design will also contribute to passive cooling strategies.

Having an effectively insulated shell that wraps the house in every direction is the first order of business. Without this isolation from the great out-of-doors, you can never expect to keep your cool; the heat will always intrude. Many houses, especially older ones, were not well insulated in the first place, so this can be a major remodeling project, depending on your specific situation. There are some books available that are devoted entirely to this topic.

One way to improve the insulation of many houses is to loosely place radiant barrier under the rafters in the attic. It needs some air space on either side to be most effective. Also, the exterior of the house can be wrapped with a radiant barrier. I did this with the manufactured home. The original exterior siding was painted pressboard that was already beginning to show its age, so I decided to both insulate the house and resurface the exterior in one operation. I stapled the radiant foil over the old siding, then tacked nailing strips over that to provide the air space between the foil and the rough-sawn siding. Ideally this space is at least 3/4 inch.

As with passive heating, a passively cooled house can benefit from having a substantial amount of thermal mass on the inside. This could be with tile or stones as I used in the Colorado house. Walls can be made with bricks or adobe. Tanks of water provide good thermal mass. Mass can be built into a variety of features inside your house, such as a stove or fireplace surround, a staircase, a decorative wall, a pond or water fountain, or a pedestal for an island counter.

The role that thermal mass plays for both heating and cooling applications is that it moderates indoor temperatures. In other words, you are much less likely to experience wide extremes of temperature, because the mass will absorb the excess coolness or heat.

If it cools off sufficiently at night during the hot season, one simple strategy is to open windows and allow the night air to penetrate the house and sweep away as much excess heat as possible. Strategically placed fans can assist with this process. Then when early morning starts to bring more heat, you can close the windows and let your thermal mass help keep the house cooler all day long.

If you happen to have a basement that is noticeably cooler than the rest of the house, it is possible to force this cooler air upstairs with a venting system that scoops up the cooler air near the floor of the basement and sends it to the floors above. This will likely require some way for the warmer air upstairs to return to the basement so there is effective circulation.

With some remodels it might be possible to create basement-like conditions without actually having an existing basement. You can berm soil up against a wall so that it effectively becomes underground. If you do this around enough of the space, you can take advantage of the relatively stable underground temperatures that exist everywhere. A yard or two below the surface will be close to the average temperature of the area year round, and it will remain at that temperature most of the time. This can provide a tremendous buffering effect on the temperatures within a house. This is the reason why water pipes are buried deep in the ground to avoid freezing.

We needed a utility room for the washer and dryer and wanted some more pantry space, so we added a room to the back of our house in Olympia, Washington. Below is a view of the house after we remodeled it to create the extra room and a covered porch area. To the left of the sliding glass entry door you can see the grass growing on the substantial berm up against that wall. The berm actually continued around to the

other side of the house, even though you can't see that in the photo.

The wall itself was built with patterned concrete blocks mortared into place with standard cinder block methods; it was made very secure with steel-reinforced concrete inside the blocks. The interior appearance is shown at the top of the photo above. On the outside, before the berm was put there, the block was thoroughly coated with a moisture-proof membrane. If this had been living space I would have also insulated the wall on the outside, similar to what I had done with the foundation wall of the garage remodel. For the floor, I acquired some surplus terracotta tile in a bunch of different sizes. I decided it

would be kind of fun to try making a mosaic tiled pattern with these. You can see the look of it in that same photo. This did require the use of a tile saw to cut some of the smaller pieces to fit it all together.

Another approach to keeping cooler is to install adequate vents and fans in an attic space that is overheating. This will effectively exhaust this heat before it can penetrate to the rooms below.

Having light-colored, reflective roofing can help a great deal in keeping temperatures from building up in an attic or room below.

Landscaping can also help keep houses cooler. Trees and shrubs can be planted to encourage prevailing winds to enter the house. Or deciduous trees can be planted to shade a house during the hot summer, and then allow more sunlight to penetrate during the winter when they have dropped their leaves. This idea can even be employed with conventional passive solar installations when the trees are planted south of the solar windows.

If you live in a dry enough climate, evaporative coolers are quite effective in cooling interior space. The concept is really quite simple: when you blow air through or past a body of water causing it to evaporate, the process of evaporation draws heat from the air, thus cooling it. Unfortunately this won't work if the air is too humid. Portable evaporative coolers are inexpensive and widely available.

Usually it is recommended that evaporative coolers are situated where they can draw in air from the outside, and they may need another window open a bit to get proper air flow. If your climate allows it, evaporative coolers use much less energy than air conditioners because all they need is a fan to to blow air through a damp membrane.

This same concept can be used by arranging the proper architectural features to encourage natural evaporation. I have seen designs that show a pool of water located near a vented wall and then another vent placed up high on the opposite wall to encourage air movement in the room.

This can be enhanced by creating what is called a "windcatcher." These have been perfected in the Middle East where hot and dry is the norm. Windcatchers usually consist of small towers or chimneys that rise above the top of a roof and they literally catch the wind, if it exists, and force it into the home, thus moving confined air out another vent or window. If there is a water feature connected to the wind catcher this can enhance the cooling effect.

Other windcatcher designs merely create a suction by diverting incoming air around an interior baffle, thus drawing out more air from inside the house. Either way you get air movement, which in itself can make you feel cooler, even if the air temperature doesn't change.

An uncommon way to take advantage of the cooler temperatures beneath the ground is to force your incoming air to travel through the ground before it enters your house. This can be done with buried vent pipes that run a long enough distance to cool the air as it travels from the inlet many yards from your home.

Your House Can Power Your Life

I love solar electricity. There is something so elegantly simple in the way photovoltaic panels silently convert sunlight directly into electrical current. There are no moving parts, just a flow of electrons moving in one direction and eventually doing electrical work. Of course there are plenty of elements that must be arranged properly before that power can actually be used, so a complete solar electrical installation can be rather complex.

My first opportunity to play with PV panels was when I installed a small system on the bus conversion motor home that I built in 1995. This bus is described in detail in my book *Rolling Shelter*. Most of the time, we relied exclusively on solar power for all of our electrical needs, so we didn't install a noisy generator in the bus. This system employed four 75 watt panels (mounted on the roof of the bus) that charged a bank of 6 deep cycle batteries. From there the electricity was either used for 12 volt DC circuits or run through a 3,000 watt inverter that changed it into regular 120 volt AC power.

This whetted my appetite for solar power sufficiently that when I built the domed earthbag house that we designed, solar panels had a prominent role. You can see how eight 75 watt PV panels were arranged at the top of the central roof. Below them are four large solar thermal panels, which provided domestic hot water, heated a hot tub, and even helped heat the second floor office located behind them.

The PV system charged a set of batteries, and the inverted AC power supplied current to some select circuits that ran all of the lights in the house as well as our refrigerator/freezer. All of the other circuits were powered from the grid. This meant that we always had some electricity available, even if the grid was down. In fact, on a few occasions, we didn't even realize that the grid power was down.

Later, when we moved into the manufactured home, we knew that we would install a PV system large enough to power the entire house. The photo at right shows all of those panels soaking up sunshine on our roof.

Before I could begin to install this system, I put a new metal roof on the house. I knew that once the panels were mounted up there I wouldn't want to do roof maintenance, and metal roofs can last for decades.

The first step in designing a PV system that will supply all of the electricity that you need is to calculate what your needs really are. If you are already connected to grid power, your monthly electric bill can give you an accurate measure of how much you have been using. Often the bill will show a graph of each month's usage over a period of one year in kilowatt hours (KWH) consumed. You can use this information to calculate how many KWH's you average per day over the course of a year. In our case we had been using about 13 KWH per day as an average over the year, so I knew that I wanted to at least cover that in designing my system.

Had I not been connected to the grid and if I needed to rely entirely on the electricity I could produce, then my strategy would have been different. In that case I would need to assure that the system could handle the highest peak month of usage, which in my case would have been about 22 KWH per day. So you can see that a stand alone system might need to be capable of producing twice as much electricity as a grid-tied one to serve the same household. This is one reason why I encourage folks to set up a net-metering grid tied system whenever practical. Not only will it save you money on the initial cost of the system, but it will be more ecological because every bit of electricity that your system produces will be used somewhere, whether it is by you or your neighbors.

Stand alone systems frequently are idle even though they could be producing electricity.

Once you have ascertained how much electricity you have been using, you might realistically look at whether you really need that much, or are there ways where your usage could be more conservative? This level of evaluation can be aided by employing a meter on your various appliances to see where all that electricity is actually going. Many electric companies or even libraries will loan you a simple device called a Kill A Watt meter, or they can be purchased for between $20 and $30. If you plug the meter into an outlet and then plug your appliance, or a power strip of several appliances, into the meter, it will give you a readout over time of how much is being consumed.

This sort of evaluation is critical with stand-alone systems, because not only will you be paying for the panels and associated electronics, but you will also need to provide a battery bank that can supply all of your electrical needs, even during overcast weather and at night. This is another reason why grid-tied sys-tems are so attractive... you don't necessarily rely on batteries which tend to be expensive and often need maintenance or replacement.

In my case I wanted the assurance that even if the grid power were out, that I would still have some electricity. So I also installed a small bank of bat-teries that could tide me through a day or two of not having the grid. Most of the time the batteries just sit unused, but they are kept well charged by my system automatically, so they will last a very long time. Also, I chose maintenance free gel cell batteries so I really don't need to pay much attention to them. They sit quietly ready to jump into service if the grid happens to go down.

Our highest consumer of electricity by far is an electric hot tub, a luxury that we supremely enjoy, particularly in this frigid climate with only three frost free months each year.

Once I had calculated that my average daily use of electricity was 13 KWH, I could figure out what size system we would need to handle this. Since the sun only shines so many hours each day, and the intensity varies according to the time of the day and the season, it can be tricky to know how big a system you really need. An estimate of the number of hours per day of good sun might be an average, at my location, of perhaps only about 5 hours. If this were true, I would need a system that could produce at least 2.6 KW (13KW divided by 5) to provide all of the electricity I needed.

PV panels are rated for a certain number of watts that they can generate when in the full sun. Of course because the sun keeps moving and the angle of the sun affects their output, they rarely produce their maximum potential. Given all of these variables, I decided to shoot for a system that would give me about 3.5 KW of power to assure that I would have plenty. I certainly had no objection to producing more than I use, since that would give me some security for future lifestyle changes and other contingencies. Also I knew that with the net metering arrangement available with the power company where I live, they would pay me back for any power that was sent back into the grid over the course of a year.

I next looked at the possible space on my roof where the panels might be located. I might have opted to place the panels on free-standing pedestals near the house, but I preferred for aesthetic and practical reasons to mount them high on my roof, out of the way.

Some of the largest panels available these days are rated for about 240 watts, and these measure about 3 by 4 feet. Using this size of panel, it would take 15 of them to come up to 3.6 KW of potential power. I carefully measured the space available up there and came up with a plan. It would cover most of the available space, without sticking the panels too high above the ridgeline of the roof or impinging on existing vents or skylights. It would also leave enough space for a small solar thermal system for our domestic hot water.

I conferred with a local solar electric systems installer and he agreed that my estimates and calculations were reasonable. He then came up with a detailed list of all of the other components that would be needed to complete the system I imagined. I placed an order for all of this through his company, as he quoted good prices and would be available for advice as necessary during the installation process. The total cost of the

entire system in 2011 was about $12,000, with me doing all of the installation. The system would also qualify for a federal tax credit, so some of that money could be recouped over time.

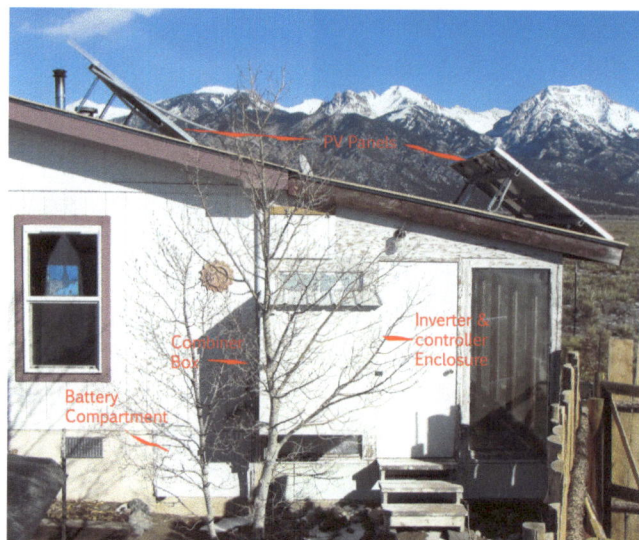

The above photo shows the basic configuration of the components, with the panels on the roof, a weather-tight enclosure for the inverter and charge controller, a box just outside that enclosure combining all of the separate feeds from the PV panels with a master cutoff switch, and a compartment under the house for the batteries.

I decided to place the inverter and its associated equipment in its own enclosure outside of the house partly because there was no other good place for them inside, but also I knew that the inverter makes noise and I didn't want to be listening to it inside. The master cutoff switch for the solar panels had to be easily thrown in case of emergency, a requirement of the power company before they would accept the system to be grid tied. The batteries conveniently were located behind an existing access door to the crawl space beneath the house. They would be totally out of the weather, safe from freezing, and close enough to the other equipment for the cables to not be too long; this is important because battery cables are huge and costly.

It was a relative short run for the conduit with the wires from the PV panels on the roof to connect with the combiner box, so the whole design was fairly compact, which is always a good thing when working with electrical circuits where wire size is partly determined by distance between connections.

This photo shows the arrangement of equipment inside the inverter's box. The inverter itself is the large column on the left. This is an Outback inverter designed specifically for my configuration. It can handle 3.6 KW of power and is set up for 48 volts of incoming DC power from the array on the roof. To the right of the inverter is the charge controller that senses the needs of the battery bank and controls grid intertie functions. Above the controller is a distribution box for communication among all of the components. Originally there was a readout and programing device mounted between those last two pieces of equipment, but I moved it to a remote location in my office just inside the house where I could monitor and control the whole system.

The conduits at the upper left of the photo connect to the incoming grid power and directly to the main breaker panel for the house. Below that is a ground wire connected to the grounding rod for the entire system (including the PV panels). The large diameter conduit on the lower left contains the cables going down to connect with the batteries (which are wired for a 48 volt system). The curved conduit comes from the combiner box and the master cutoff switch for the incoming DC power.

The large inverter enclosure has a door and a roof that keeps out all weather, is insulated to help keep it

from overheating, and is vented for the same reason. This equipment is much more sensitive to heat than to cold, so I have to monitor the temperature in there, especially during the warm season.

The entirety of this installation had to be inspected by our state electrical inspector to make sure that it met all of the codes. The inspector gave me a green light the first time around, so I was quite pleased with that. Then an inspector from the power company had to check it out, making sure that the quality of the inverted power met their specs as well, which it did, so then they installed a special meter used for net metering.

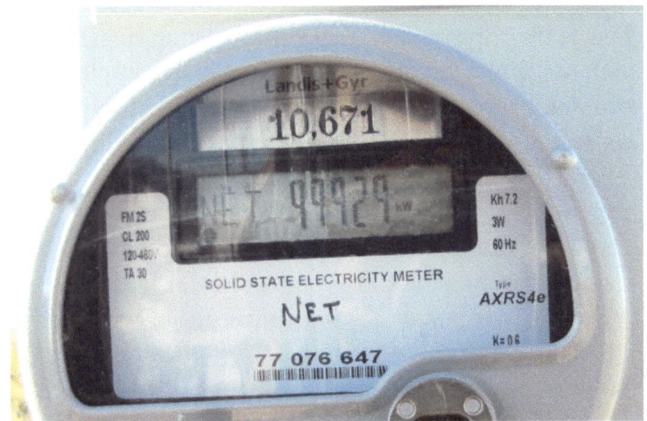

This photo was taken some time after they installed the meter. The reading at that time was 99929 KWH's. Since the meter was set at 00000 when it was installed, this would indicate that the meter had been running backwards enough over the time since it was installed to credit me with 71 KWH worth of electricity. How nice!

Over the few years that this system has been functioning, we have consistently had a positive balance on our account with the power company. This has led us to seriously consider using this extra electricity to charge a plug-in electric car. When we looked into this we found that it is possible to convert some of the older Prius hybrid vehicles to be plug-ins as well as hybrid gas/electric vehicles. So now we have exchanged our old gas vehicle for a used Prius and we may add the extra battery pack and electronics to be able to charge it with our own renewable energy. Then we could do most of our driving totally carbon free. The range of the added battery is about 30 miles, but most of our driving is local and easily within that range, so this is quite feasible.

This is the little solar thermal array set up to assist with our domestic hot water. It is a fairly simple system that heats the water that is stored directly in our hot water tank. There are no other tanks employed, so it hardly takes up any extra space in our house.

The fluid running through these panels to be heated is not water, however. It is a kind of non-toxic glycol because water would obviously freeze and burst the pipes and rupture the panels. In climates where freezing is not a danger, the water can be circulated directly from the panels and into the hot water tank. But in our case, we needed to use a heat exchanger between two circuits, one for antifreeze and one for water. Some solar thermal panels are designed so that the water can be drained back into a small tank located where it won't freeze when the pump is not circulating. With these drain-back systems you don't need to use the glycol and the heat exchanger, so they can be more efficient.

There are two little DC in-line pumps that cause the water and glycol to circulate. Each pump is connected to its own small PV panel on the roof of the house. This simple concept means that the only time the fluids circulate is if the sun is shining, and the rate of the circulation is determined by how strong the sun is. No switching or monitoring of the system is needed on a regular basis.

This is what the heat exchanger looks like. The two fluids never touch; they are always separated by thin metal plates that actually transfer heat from the solar panel to the domestic hot water. All of the tubing used in the system is surrounded by insulation to conserve the heat. The valves you can see in the picture were used to initially charge the system with glycol. Behind them is visible a small expansion tank needed to allow the fluid to expand and contract as necessary. And it is all pressurized a bit as well.

If you happen to have running water on your property, or if you have consistent winds to harness, micro hydro and wind generators may be practical for your situation. There is a long history of these technologies and they are quite practical in the right situations. There is much more information about them on my website.

Water is the Essence of Life

Water makes it all possible; without it we are in big trouble. This chapter is about assuring that there is always a supply of water on hand, potable and otherwise. Conserving the water that is available is clearly the best strategy for sustainable living. And increasing the supply where possible also makes sense.

I have created rainwater catchment systems on two of the houses I have remodeled, and this can be a great way to collect usable water that would otherwise just seep back into the earth. The first such system was in Olympia, Washington.

We realized that it would be possible to put a water storage tank in the berm that I had created behind the wall of the utility space I had built. Simple gutters could collect all of the rainwater off of the north side of the house and the garage and dump it into the tank, and since the tank would be underground it would be protected from freezing in that climate.

As part of our water conservation measures we eliminated a large part of the lawn that covered our back yard, and replaced it with gravel, decorative bricks and some selected ground covering plants that would not need to be watered. In doing this, we also created a driveway leading to the back yard and an eventual garage. The blocks of sod we dug up to remove the lawn were stacked up as a slightly inclined wall to retain the berm. This shows in the above photo as green grass, since the exposed grass continued to grow!

In this photo you can see that same scene after the garage was built. I used similar concrete blocks to build the walls of the garage as I had used on the utility room. I coated the area that would be bermed with waterproofing compound, then stacked more blocks of sod as a retaining wall. The soil that was dug out to create a hole for recessing the water tank was thrown up against the garage wall.

The tank held about 500 gallons and was designed for direct burial. It had inlet and outlet ports up high at either end. You can see how I connected pipes to the inlet port that ran from both the house and the other side of the garage where they would collect rainwater from gutters on both buildings. There is another unseen pipe that exits the tank near its base, goes through the berm, and has a spigot attached for connecting a hose. This is how the water could be used for irrigating the garden or the tank could be drained.

The finished installation is pictured above. We collected rocks to make a waterfall from any water that overflowed the tank when it was full. This really only happened when it was raining. That water would cascade into a small pond dug at the base of the rock work. From the pond there was a buried pipe running across the driveway to a small drain field that would absorb any overflowing water. We stocked the pond with goldfish, and they were quite happy in there. The wire fence at the top of the berm was to keep our dogs from climbing onto the roof.

This provided a pleasant spot for us to sit under the porch roof and watch the waterfall when it rained. I also installed a little recirculating pump that allowed us to watch the waterfall any time we wanted, just by throwing a switch.

Our intention was to only use this water for irrigating our garden or trees and other plants in the yard, so there was no filtration system. We had wire mesh over the drains in the gutters to keep leaves and debris from entering the tank.

Our little homestead in Colorado has provided anoth-

er opportunity to install a rainwater catchment system. The climate is much more arid, so the chances to collect rainwater are fewer, but the scarcity of water generally makes the proposition even more attractive.

We decided to build a barn/garage complex that has a recessed pantry on its north side. Within the pantry we thought we would include a large water reservoir, expecting that it would not only provide an extra water supply, but would also help stabilize the temperatures in the pantry, keeping it from freezing during our long winters and helping to keep it cooler during the summer. Part of the idea was to collect rainwater from the nearly 1,000 square foot roof area and dump it into the water tank.

The roofing material that we used was metal, the same as what was used to reroof the main house. Metal roofs make good rainwater catchment surfaces because they do not impart any toxic impurities to the water and they tend to be fairly clean.

The pantry was dug down about six feet under the ground and the walls were shored up by just filling polypropylene bags with the native sand dug out of

We planned to buy a water tank that might hold 800 gallons because we didn't want it to take up too much space in the pantry. But then we found an unused tank of 1550 gallons that had been stored in a garage for many years at a price we couldn't refuse ($300) so we decided to buy it. You can see this tank on its side in the photo, waiting to be lowered into the pantry hole.

Below is an exterior view of the finished pantry with cordwood walls elevated above grade. We chose this method of wall building because it provides good insulation (the walls are 15 inches thick and have a hollow insulating core filled with sawdust and lime), it is inexpensive and looks great.

There will be a gutter along the back of the barn that collects water off of the roof and funnels it through a pipe in the wall and on down to the tank. As a kind of filter, a simple reservoir will hold the first several gallons of water that comes off the roof before the cleaner water will be allowed to enter the tank. This reservoir will be dumped after each storm so it is ready for the next one. There will be a float valve that keeps the tank from overflowing.

the hole. These walls were inclined outward so there was no impulse for them to collapse inward. The black plastic in the above photo lined the walls on the outside to keep moisture from intruding. This plastic also helped keep the bags out of the sun during construction, because the UV in sunlight will quickly degrade the polypropylene.

This stored water will mostly be used for outdoor watering, but in an emergency we might need to filter it for domestic use. Since the tank is below ground level, the water will need to be pumped for use, but at least with our solar electric system we are guaranteed to have electricity for pumping.

Speaking of emergency water storage, it is recommended that any home have one gallon of potable water available for every person in the household per day. And there should be enough to last at least three days. This is just for drinking and cooking; you also need some water on hand to flush toilets, clean dishes, bathe, etc. Another gallon per person per day would be a minimal amount to have on hand for emergency situations.

There is always the possibility that algae or bacteria could develop in a tank of stored water, especially if light reaches the water. To avoid this some folks add a bit of bleach or food grade hydrogen peroxide periodically. If you want to try this I recommend doing some research on recommended dosages and treatment periods. Further research will inform you about filtration or purification equipment that can be used to make potable water out of some pretty vile stuff, including water containing bacteria or viruses.

Another approach to water conservation is the use of compost toilets. They don't consume any water at all and are one the the most ecological ways of dealing with human waste. We have used compost toilets in three different situations.

Our first experience was at our family commune at Sunshine Camp, where we started out using the communal toilet facility which was a bit of a hike to access. As we contemplated having our own bathroom next to our bedroom, we considered various ways to have a toilet. Some of the other houses on the property had their own septic systems, but this wasn't very appealing to us, as there was no convenient place to locate a leach field.

When I ran across the Swedish Clivus Multrum composting system I thought this might be ideal for our situation. The concept was rather simple: there were no moving parts nor electricity used, it required minimal maintenance, the composting was aerobic so there would be no methane gas to deal with, the design created a downdraft at the toilet seat so noxious fumes were minimal, and there was a separate hatch

for collecting finished compost about once a year. The only hitch was that the commercial models were quite expensive. So I decided to try my hand at building my own.

Usually they are made from molded fiberglass or plastic, but I figured that I could fabricate the same design with concrete, plywood, and plastic pipe. The design calls for a base that is inclined at about 30 degrees so that the composting material tends to slide downward by gravity. As it travels downward and forward toward the finish chamber, the material becomes aerated through contact with a manifold system of small pipes bringing oxygen from the outside air. The whole concept is quite brilliant.

First I dug a hole about the right size below where the toilet seat would be located in the eventual bathroom. I inclined the bottom of the hole at the proper angle, and made forms to be able to pour concrete that would line the entire basin with about 6 inches of concrete. The above photo shows the concrete basin, with the large opening where finished compost would be gathered; a hatch would cover the finish chamber. There was a wooden baffle between the two chambers in the tank that kept the uncomposted material from entering the finish tank too soon, as there was an open space of only about 6 inches beneath the baffle.

The upper part of the arrangement was built with plywood coated with urethane to protect it from the moisture. Visible in the photo are three holes cut in this plywood enclosure, but there is actually one other large diameter hole cut in the uppermost panel. The lower small pipe protruding above the plywood was the air inlet for the aeration system, and this was screened to keep insects from entering. The large diameter hole was intended for dumping kitchen scraps and other compostable materials. You can see in the photo below how that was accessed via a special chute above the deck (it has the potted plant on it.)

The next pipe going vertically out of the chamber was the primary exhaust for the entire toilet. This exhaust pipe was actually two pipes nested within each other, so that the inner pipe was insulated somewhat from the atmosphere. The idea was that the heat generated by the composting material would rise to the highest level of the upper chamber, and thus go up the exhaust vent by convection, aided by the warmer interior pipe. This process of convection was also aided by the turban cap I put on top of the large exterior metal pipe, up above the roof. Any breeze would draw air out of the exhaust vent.

The toilet itself is shown in the above photo with the large diameter pedestal sticking above the deck. I found some stainless steel cylinders of about 14" diameter that I used for both the toilet and the other compost chutes. I made the toilet seat from some nice solid oak boards laminated together, cut to the right shape, and coated with urethane. There was a rubber gasket between the toilet seat and the hinged lid that kept insects from entering.

In practice the system worked pretty well, with just few problems. The venting system was great, and really kept objectionable odors from being a problem. We did occasionally have a few flies find their way into the tank and multiply, despite all of our precautions. The most difficult problem to deal with was that somehow groundwater leached into the concrete tank, most likely from a seam in the concrete. The

excess moisture flooded the base of the finish tank which disturbed the composting process and made it messy to deal with.

It was really too late to consider trying to seal the tank from either the inside or the outside. As a solution to this problem I dug down into the earth at the lower end of the concrete and drilled a hole through the concrete wall near the base of the finish compartment. I placed a hose through the hole into the tank and sealed it into place, then ran that hose to connect with a small leach field we had already installed to deal with gray water from our kitchen and bathroom sinks and the old fashioned bathtub in the bathroom. This did adequately drain the tank, so all was well again.

The other compost toilets we have experienced were both smaller commercial models. One of these we installed in our bus conversion motor home, both to conserve water use and to eliminate the need for a black water tank. This toilet was really quite small, being sized to fit into the hull of a small sail boat. It was, however rated for two people to be able to use.

There was a small fan that helped force air out of the vent pipe, so it wasn't particularly odorous. The main problem we had with this system is that it was really too small for us living full time in the motor home, so that we overwhelmed its capacity before the compost was finished and ready to be removed. This meant that we had to manually clean out the toilet too soon, which was not a pleasant job!

This toilet had an electric heater that we sometimes used to help speed the composting process along, but since we generally relied on the solar panels to provide the electricity we used, there was not generally enough power to use the heater.

We also had to install a special tank to collect excess urine because it did not evaporate quickly enough, and that tank had to be drained periodically. All-in-all, our experience with this little compost toilet was not very positive.

The final compost toilet we had was in Mexico. Our house was connected to the sewer, but we had a small motor home that became our casita for guests, parked at the other end of the property. The RV had its own little toilet and black water tank, but there was no convenient way to dump it without driving somewhere else. When we noticed a classified ad for a commercial compost toilet for sale, we checked it out as a way to provide a toilet facility for guests. It was basically new, never having been used because it didn't fit into the space that the owner thought it would. We bought it for a good price and set it up in its own little booth next to the RV. This toilet was much larger than the previous one, and would only see occasional use, so we figured it would work fine... which it did.

As a final word about compost toilets, I would advise you that all of them require a certain degree of acceptance of natural, earthy processes. You might be able to see or smell the feces occasionally, and the finished compost does have to be cleaned out periodically. If you enjoy gardening and making your own compost and spreading it onto your soil, then you might be a candidate for being a happy compost toilet owner. If all of this makes you squeamish, then compost toilets may not be for you.

Another water conservation measure has to do with what happens to the gray water that exits your house via drain pipes. Typically this water is simply com-

bined with the black water from the toilets and sent to either the sewer or a septic system. This is unfortunate though, since the gray water could be reused to help water outdoor plants. Some people devise separate branched drain systems that divert the gray water for reuse.

Any water the comes from a shower or bath tub, or from bathroom sinks is a candidate for this. Water from toilets, kitchen sinks and clothes washing machines may contain suspect contaminants and regulations often exclude it from being diverted for reuse. The clothes washer might be cleaning baby diapers, and that is why it is excluded. The kitchen sink might have bacteria supporting waste in it.

When we needed to deal with gray water from our bathroom and kitchen at Sunshine Camp, we installed a simple leach field arrangement to take care of it. This was not technically reusing it, as it didn't really water any specific plants, but it was a way of dealing with it. One thing we did was install what is called a "grease trap." This was a mostly buried bucket with an inlet near the top from the kitchen sink. The outlet that led to the leach field had an elbow in the pipe that allowed only the water from the bottom of the bucket to enter. The idea was that then any grease or oil would float on top of the water and not clog the rest of the drain system. This did work effectively; all we needed to do is periodically clean any collected grease off the top of the trap and dispose of it otherwise.

There are many other water saving devices and appliances that can be employed in your house. One that we have tried is a front loading clothes washing machine. These typically use much less water and soap than the top loaders, and they get the clothes just as clean. Some people contrive ways to use gray water from an adjacent sink to flush the toilet, and this makes sense. Low-flow shower heads and aerated sink nozzles are other possibilities. And of course common toilets have options for minimal water use for flushing these days, some having a dual flush choice depending on need. It behooves us all to conserve water as much as possible, so we will continue to have enough to go around for everybody.

Using Natural and Recycled Materials

Sustainable architecture has a lot to do with the materials that are employed to build with. This is because they can have such a huge impact on energy usage, health, comfort, building longevity and ecosystems.

One rule of thumb is the more local the material is, the better. This is because transportation has such a large impact on greenhouse gas production, fossil fuel consumption and the cost of materials. Also, local natural materials often seem to fit better in any particular environment.

In Mexico when we chose to cover the ceiling of our new sunroom with reed mats, these just felt right since they were locally made. Had we insisted on using sheetrock for this project, like a lot of foreigners would have, this likely would have been imported from the United States. At the rental in Bernal, when we used palm fronds to shade the sunroom roof, these fit in perfectly with the feeling of the place. Not only were they local and natural, but they were also recycled; we found them at a church, about to be tossed away after Palm Sunday.

More recently, when we chose to use log rounds from dead trees in the nearby forest for the cordwood masonry project, these seem to fit the character of this place naturally. So do the stone foundation and rough sawn boards and batts cut from beetle killed trees that we used to build our barn complex.

Another rule of thumb is that natural, rather than industrial, materials are preferable. The reasons for this are numerous. A lot of it has to do with embodied energy. Industrial materials first have to be sourced and transported from the place where they are dug up, or otherwise accessed, to the factory where they are converted to the product. All of this takes energy, which most likely means fossil fuel consumption and air pollution. Complex products often move from one factory to another, multiplying the embodied energy even further. Then there is the marketing necessary to get that product into your hands, which may involve several warehouses and other vehicular trips, as well as packaging, labeling and all the rest, increasing the embodied energy.

Compare this to digging up soil in your yard or collecting some nearby stones and moving them in a wheelbarrow for use in your project, where there is virtually no embodied energy other than a bit of your own sweat.

With the wood I used to build my barn/garage pictured above, there certainly is some embodied energy, but it is limited to the work of one local logger who cut and hauled the beetle killed trees from a nearby forest to his home sawmill. The logs were passed through his saw a few times to slice them into usable planks, and then stacked on his trailer to be hauled the few miles to my house, where we unloaded them by hand. Compared to what most industrial materials go through, this lumber has minimal embodied energy.

There is another level of preference for using natural, rather than industrial, materials that is worth mentioning, and it has to do with our health. Most unprocessed, natural materials that might be used for building are completely benign. Certainly there is nothing toxic about the stones or the soil or the wood mentioned so far. The same goes for straw bales, bamboo, and many other natural materials commonly used in building.

Many industrial materials often used in houses carry hidden threats to our health. For instance the formaldehyde used in manufacturing press board may take several years to completely off gas. New carpets may impart noxious fumes for a surprisingly long time. The cumulated effect of these sorts of hazards has been called "sick building syndrome" and has been recognized as a modern health problem. Our environment is so burdened these days with contaminants from so many sources, why bring these into your home as well?

After we bought the manufactured home in Colorado we realized that there were a number of elements that we wanted to change. One of these was the cabinet doors in the kitchen because they were made from pressboard with a fake wood-grain plastic coating. The plastic was wearing thin and the doors looked really tacky. When I picked up some blue-stained beetle-killed pine boards that were sold to me as firewood, I knew that I couldn't just burn them in the wood stove. Instead I pieced the rustic wood together and made new cabinet doors in the kitchen. This completely transformed the feeling of the kitchen from fake to genuine... what a transformation! The cabinets behind the doors were still the same old pressboard, but we figured that the house was old enough that they had stopped off gassing, and it would have been a huge project to replace them, so we decided to keep them.

I am not a total purist about not using industrial materials. In many instances there simply are no functional alternatives to their use. It is all about moderation. For instance, Portland cement has very high embodied energy, but it definitely has a reasonable

place as a material for use in natural building. I use it in the mortar for stonework or cordwood masonry and I use it to pour concrete piers for wooden posts. But I avoid intensive uses such as pouring large basement foundations because I have found other, more benign ways to do this sort of thing.

I have worked with wood all my life, first in my father's cabinet shop and later as a carpenter remodeling houses. I love wood and what it can do. But I also love forests and the ecosystems that they support and want to protect these extremely important places on Earth.

When I lived in the Pacific Northwest I witnessed firsthand the utter destruction that modern forestry practices can wreak on our environment. It is heartbreaking to see a forest that supports so much life having been transformed into a wasteland seemingly bereft of life. And the loss of habitat is mirrored by the loss of trees that can scrub carbon dioxide from our air... a double whammy. All of this to supply the United State's gluttonous appetite for wood-framed houses.

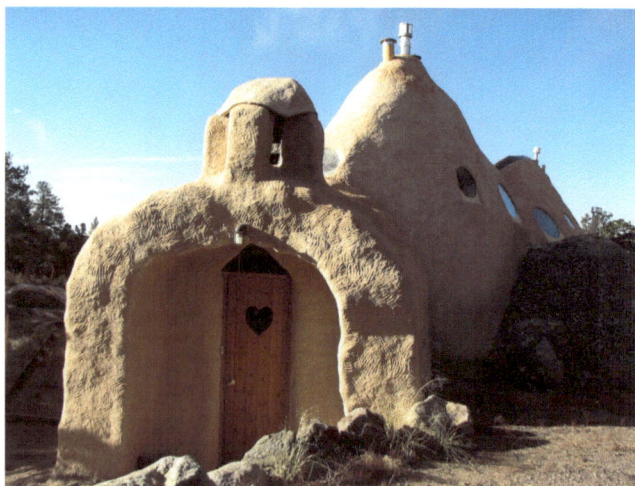

When we decided to build our own house we used as little wood as possible, making domes with earthbags instead, and either harvesting standing dead timbers or using recycled wood where needed. Building this house is chronicled in another book I'm writing specifically about my involvement with earthbag building.

You can use wood with a good conscience if you carefully research where it comes from and how it has been harvested. Homes can be made with certi-

fied sustainably harvested trees. This means that the forests where the trees are harvested are monitored to make sure that the health and character of the forest is maintained. Only certain trees are culled periodically, leaving the remaining trees to grow and contribute to a healthy ecosystem.

Unfortunately, the American Forest and Paper Industries has begun to mislead the public with their own SFI (Sustainable Forestry Initiative) label, which would better be considered the "Same-old Forest Industry" label. The Forest Stewardship Council (FSC) legitimately certifies forest products, so look for the FSC label.

I am a big fan of using recycled materials. It just makes so much sense from every sustainable angle. Each time you reuse materials instead of buying new ones, you are saving all of the embodied energy that was once invested in that material rather than causing more embodied energy to be consumed in the production of new materials.

The cost of acquiring recycled materials is usually considerably less than buying new ones; often they are free. I think that economics is a distinct part of sustainable living. Conservation of personal finances leads to having more money and time to devote to other important aspects of your life that can lead to more enjoyment and better health. Saving money is good for you!

When we needed a chicken coop to house our fledgling flock of chicks, I looked around to see what was

at hand to use for building this. My eyes fell upon a couple of huge rusting steel tongues that had been used to haul the two halves of our manufactured home. They had simply been left in the sand nearby after the hauling job was done. I had been stumbling on these heavy triangular shaped objects for too long, and realized that they would make perfect supports for an A-framed chicken coop.

First I made a foundation with earthbags filled with our local sand, plastered the bags to protect them from sun and beaks, and laid some boards over them as a plate to rest the A-frame onto. Then I erected a big tripod of logs to lift the tongues into place using a hand winch. The tongues were placed at either end of the foundation and then tied together with wood salvaged from a local remodeling project.

The coop was insulated with commercial EPS foam and then sheathed on the outside with metal roofing seconds I picked up from a store that sells custom roof panels. The inside was sheathed with old weathered boards salvaged from old raised garden beds. The window and door were collected by a friend who had a deconstruction business. So almost all of the materials that went into building the chicken coop were recycled, and it just cost me a few dollars to make. It will probably last a lifetime.

Later, when I integrated this coop with the large barn/garage and the mudroom that connected it to our house, I continued utilizing as much recycled material as I could. All of the windows and doors were salvaged from deconstructed houses. The main entry door and its mate had been a set of fine oak French doors, both still in good shape, only needing some refinishing. About half of the metal roofing was similar to what I used on the coop. Even though the colors didn't match, it didn't matter because the roof couldn't be seen from anywhere but an airplane. The sliding door track for the large garage doors was pieced together from sections I found at a local scrap metal yard. Only the actual rolling hardware was new. Most people when first viewing this project would not realize how much of it had been recycled, as it all just seems to fit naturally together.

The photo shows how all of this connects to the original house. As time allows I will put the same kind of board and batt treatment over the entire house, so it will all be integrated into a uniform whole. My plan is to let the natural wood just weather over time, so eventually the house will look like an old time cabin.

The original foam insulating skirting around the base of the manufactured home will be covered with natural stonework to protect it and add the look of a real stone foundation for the house.

This brings me to my last point about choosing materials and methods for remodeling: build to last! Longevity has got to be a primary goal for any sustainable building. In our throw-away culture, way too much building has been inconsiderate of the effect of time on materials and designs.

I always consider the durability of materials when choosing what to use. Obviously masonry materials, like stone or brick, will last longer than organic materials, like straw bales or wood. This is where it becomes important to look at the specific design to make sure that any materials used are done so in such a way that they are protected from decay.

Never place materials vulnerable to rot where they will regularly get wet and not be able to dry out. Wood should never touch the ground, not only because of possible rotting, but also because termites will certainly find the wood and happily eat away at it unnoticed. Many wall systems, like strawbale walls, do best if they are allowed to breathe on both sides; this allows any moisture that might find its way inside the wall to dissipate over time.

There are specific design features that should be addressed, such as venting the crawl space under a floor so that too much humidity doesn't build up in the space and promote mold or dry rot. And, as I learned with the garage remodel in Olympia, it is important to vent attic areas over any heated space. You might need professional advice about flashing details with roofs, or proper ways to install windows to avoid intrusion of moisture. These things are important if you want your house to last.

Your House Can Help Feed You

Rosana and I love to garden, and having adequate gardening space has always been a priority for us. Even in the Mexican rental house we had a spot picked out in the back yard for raising vegetables.

There is nothing as good as freshly picked produce for taste and nutritional value. The convenience of having that produce in your own garden means that you can pick it just before a meal. There is also a sense of security in having your own source of food. And, of course, the cost of doing this can be considerably less than buying produce at stores.

The sunroom that we attached to our house in Ashland, Oregon, was more intended as adjunct heat for the house than for growing things, although we did have some hanging planters in there. We did, however, create the splendid outdoor vegetable garden pictured below. We even went to the trouble of piping water to the garden from a canal above the house nearly a block away. We also had the garden set up on an automatic irrigation system, so we could leave for several days without worrying about watering the garden.

At our Mexican house, where the climate was so benign (it never froze and rarely got above about 95 degree F.), we could garden outside year round. This was a real blessing. Besides veggies, we grew our own bananas, papayas, lemons, mangos, pistachios, and lichees. Our neighbors had avocados that would occasionally drop on our side of the fence.

Olympia, Washington also had a climate that would support outdoor gardening most of the year. We created a series of raised garden beds, where we grew vegetables. The biggest problem we had to deal with there was an abundance of huge banana slugs patrolling the neighborhood. We discovered that we could

gardening energy out of doors at that time. We found that this unheated space (pictured at right) kept from freezing as long as the outdoor temperature did not dip below zero degrees F. This was with using thermal curtains at night and with the well insulated hot tub in the room as well. During the winter we tended to plant frost tolerant plants in the greenhouse.

Below is a view of our outdoor garden that was well fenced to keep out most marauders and the fierce winds that we got, especially in the spring time. The raised beds were circled with natural stones. Several of the beds have vertical wire mesh for climbing plants.

line the rim of the planter boxes with copper foil and this would deter these plant predators.

In both houses we have owned in the high mountains of Colorado, at over 8,000 feet elevation, we have needed to have covered greenhouses or cold frames to extend the growing season. With the earthbag house that we designed and built, the greenhouse was adjacent to the kitchen, so it couldn't have been more convenient. In the opposite photo the netting that is draped along the planting bed was used to keep our cats out. This greenhouse was designed to both grow plants and to heat the whole central space of the house (including the upstairs office.) We controlled the buildup of unwanted heat through sections of the glazed roofing being openable to vent heat directly, plus a section of hanging louvered curtains that could be drawn across the space. The flagstone floor served as thermal mass, as did the base of the adjacent solar hot tub.

As mentioned earlier, the manufactured home that we bought already had a custom attached greenhouse. It featured vertical glass with a substantial eave over the glass, so it didn't work well as a greenhouse during the summer, but that was fine because we moved our

We built a simple cold frame to get an early start on plants to set out into the main garden later, and also as a place to keep some plants that particularly love warmer weather. It worked very well for these purposes, providing tomatoes, cucumbers, cauliflower, squashes, peppers, eggplants and many other veggies in abundance.

One Winter Solstice we decided to experiment with planting in the cold frame just to see if was possible to use it in the winter for growing food. As a sort of control, we also planted seeds in the adjacent greenhouse at the same time. We chose mostly cool season plants, such as lettuce, arugula, peas, bok choy, kale, radishes, etc. that we knew could take a light frost.

It turned out to be particularly cold weather, with several weeks when it never got above freezing outside and with many nights in the minus teens and down to minus thirty degrees F. This, combined with the shortest days of the year, made for harsh growing conditions to say the least.

The seeds were understandably slow to germinate, but nearly all of them did eventually push their tender little feelers into the crisp air. Less than two months later, we were eating salad greens daily and peas.

The surprising thing to me is that the cold frame actually out-performed the greenhouse. Why would this be? The secret was basic passive solar design.

As you might be able to tell from the accompanying photos, the cold frame has a wall of large stones stacked against the north side, which is also the insulated foundation wall for the greenhouse. These stones absorb heat from the sun all day long (even on overcast days) and hold the heat, gently releasing it throughout the night.

Another unseen trick to the design is that I buried about two feet of inch and a half rigid insulation in the ground around the perimeter of the cold frame. This effectively isolates the frozen ground outside the cold frame from cooling the soil inside. Even when the air temperature inside the frame might go below freezing, I don't think the soil did. At night, I also placed insulation panels on top of the cold frame to help keep it toastier in there.

This cold frame is roughly 16 feet long, 3 feet wide and 2 feet high in the back, tapering to 18 inches in the front. The top is made of two lids that are hinged in the back so they can be lifted and secured up against the greenhouse wall if necessary, or propped open to ventilate the space. Depending on what you might want to grow in such a cold frame, it could be built higher to accommodate larger plants. During the summer when I had peppers and eggplants growing in the cold frame, I just left the lid open all of the time, so the plants grew beyond the height limits. The total cost of the materials for this was about $250, mostly for the 3/8 inch twin wall polycarbonate glazing.

Ordinarily, I wouldn't advise that people plant seeds in the dead of winter; had I planted earlier, we would have been enjoying salad greens much sooner. What is exciting to me about this experiment is that it proves that it is possible to grow food in extremely cold climates year round, without any heat other than that provided by the sun.

I installed a wireless thermometer gauge inside the cold frame that has a readout on my desk, where I monitor the temperature frequently. If it rises close to 100 degrees F. I will go out and prop open the top of the cold frame to allow ventilation to keep from cooking the veggies. I enjoy keeping track of this, and it is easy since I am home most of the time. But if circumstances were different, I could install a simple thermostatically controlled ventilation system to keep the cold frame from overheating.

On a frosty day when I opened the lid of the cold frame to water or harvest veggies, the steamy interior air would spill over the sides. That wonderful warm, humid environment is perfect for the little plants. They are happy… and that makes us happy!

Storing Provisions

Equally important to growing some of your own food is storing it appropriately. In this age of electric refrigeration, the use of cool storage pantries and root cellars has all but faded into oblivion. This is unfortunate, since they have great value for many reasons. There is only so much that can be put into a refrigerator, and the bigger the fridge, the more it costs to keep it cool. With pantries and root cellars, the storage potential is much greater and the cool atmosphere is free and non-polluting.

There is a distinction between a root cellar and a cool pantry: humidity. A true root cellar should be kept fairly moist in order to best preserve the crops that are stored there, whereas a pantry needs to be much dryer to avoid spoilage. Root cellars are limited in their use, but a pantry can store practically anything.

Before the days of refrigeration, root cellars and ice boxes were about the only ways to keep certain crops fresh after harvest. Root cellars were usually separate from the house and dug into the ground to take advantage of the cool, stable temperature beneath the surface.

A convenient root cellar will have a door for entry, sometimes placed flat on the ground or at an angle, but probably the best arrangement is with a vertical, insulated door. If the root cellar itself is completely underground (which it really needs to be to take advantage of the cool earth), then there would be steps that descend to the door, or a covered entrance with steps after the door. Another possibility is digging into a hillside. Depending on the stability of the soil, the sides of the excavation might either be left unfinished or lined with materials to create a retaining wall. The roof needs to be supported by some fairly massive timbers to support up to two feet of dirt placed on top. Care should be taken to avoid contact between the dirt and any wood used. Sheets of heavy polyethylene can be used to good advantage to protect the wood. Usually if the floor is left as natural earth, or just has a layer of gravel on it, the humidity will remain high enough to store most produce.

It is a good idea to provide some ventilation, with a high outlet vent and a low inlet vent. These could be closed during really cold spells to assure that nothing freezes, but having some air movement keeps the space fresh and allows off-gassing of the produce to occur without harm. Apples will give off ethylene gas which can cause potatoes to sprout prematurely and make carrots go bitter, so store the apples near the outlet vent.

We created a simple root cellar in Olympia, Washington. The open insulated door accesses an enclosed storage area that is entirely encased in the earth that is bermed against the outside of the concrete block wall. This provided a very effective and convenient way of storing produce.

If you keep a thermometer/humidity gauge in the root cellar you can monitor the space for optimal conditions and make adjustments as needed for what you are storing. Vegetables that like to be cold and very moist (33-40 degrees F., 90-95% humidity) include: carrots, beets, celery, Chinese cabbage, kohlrabi, Brussels sprouts, rutabagas, turnips, collards, broccoli and Jerusalem artichokes. Produce that likes to be kept cold and fairly moist (33-40 degrees F., 80-90% humidity) include: potatoes, cabbage, cauliflower, apples, grapes, oranges, pears and grapefruit. Produce that likes to be kept cool and fairly moist (40-45 degrees F., 85-90% humidity) include: cucumbers, sweet peppers, cantaloupe, watermelon, eggplant and ripe tomatoes. Vegetables that prefer cool and dry conditions (35-40 degrees F., 60-70% humidity) include garlic and onions. Produce that likes to be stored in fairly warm, dry conditions (50-60 degrees F., 60-70% humidity) include: dry hot peppers, pumpkins, winter squash, sweet potatoes and green tomatoes.

Unless you have an abundance of the produce mentioned above, a root cellar may not be so useful for you. On the other hand, a cool pantry would be useful for almost anybody. We built one as an extension of our earthbag house and would have felt deprived without it. We decided to make a rather large one (about 100 square feet). This allowed us to keep lots of staples on hand, which diminished our need to make trips out to stock up on food, and it's a great feeling to know that we could survive all manner of problems and help our neighbors as well.

Our pantry was situated right next to our kitchen, which made it especially useful. Most food items will last much longer if kept cool and dry, so we had grains, beans, nuts, dried produce, dry milk, canned goods, pet food, wine, etc., much of it in 5-gallon containers. There was lots of room in there to store empty bottles and miscellaneous kitchen wares that we didn't need frequently. We didn't have a separate root cellar, so we also stored fruit, potatoes, garlic and onions, yams and squash in there. These items definitely lasted much longer than they would have at room temperature in our kitchen.

This pantry was dug about five feet into the ground on the north side of the house. It was semi-circular

in shape, with sloping walls made of polypropylene bags filled with sand at the lower level and crushed volcanic rock above that. The conical roof was partially supported with a pole framework because the pitch was too shallow for the bags to be self-supporting. The whole thing was just covered with several layers of plastic sheeting and then covered entirely with dirt. There was an inlet air vent on one side and an outlet vent at the very top. The floor was adobe poured over plastic sheeting, so the atmosphere was fairly dry. After quite a few afternoon rains, the humidity in there was only 64%. It never leaked. The temperature ranged from a low of about 36 degrees F. (in the dead of winter) to a high of about 65 degrees F. in the heat of the summer. If it were dug deeper into the ground this spread would have been less.

At our little homestead with the manufactured home, we also wanted to have a naturally cooled pantry and eventually designed one into the barn/garage complex. I've already explained how we put a large water storage tank in that same room.

We needed to have a deep trench dug with a backhoe for a frostless hydrant in the barn, so we decided to also have a hole dug for the recessed pantry at the same time. We wanted ample space to accommodate a water tank and lots of cool storage, so the hole measured roughly 15 by 15 feet. Rather than dig down the entire intended depth of six feet, I had the hole dug down only about four feet. This was to allow extra dirt (sand in this case) at the bottom of the hole to use to fill earthbags for building the retaining walls around the pantry.

I inclined the bags of sand outward as they got higher, so that they would better serve as retaining walls. In fact they were sufficiently inclined that I didn't even bother placing barbed wire between the courses of bags, as it seemed unlikely that there would be any impulse to shift once they were stabilized with backfilled soil. I did place barbed wire between the bags on the wall that was adjacent to the garage, not wanting the weight and force of traffic in there to put any distorting pressure on that wall.

At the very beginning of building the walls I placed large sheets of black polyethylene between the bags and the berm. This served both to keep moisture from intruding into the space and to cover the bags during the construction process, keeping the sunlight off them.

Near the floor level I inserted a section of 6 inch PVC pipe with an elbow going up the back and more pipe

extending above grade. This was to create an inlet air vent for the pantry.

By the time that I got all of the bag walls in place I had used up all of the extra soil at the bottom of the hole. I had even started using the extra sand piled up from the original excavation.

In order to calculate exactly how to frame the roof I needed a precise plan for how the space would be used. Since I had purchased such a large water storage tank, this became rather critical. I used Sketchup, the free design software provided by Google, to figure out an appropriate design, and what I came up with is shown below.

Above the water tank there would be a deck that one entered onto from the garage. Lots of built-in shelves would be accessible from this deck. Then a spiral-

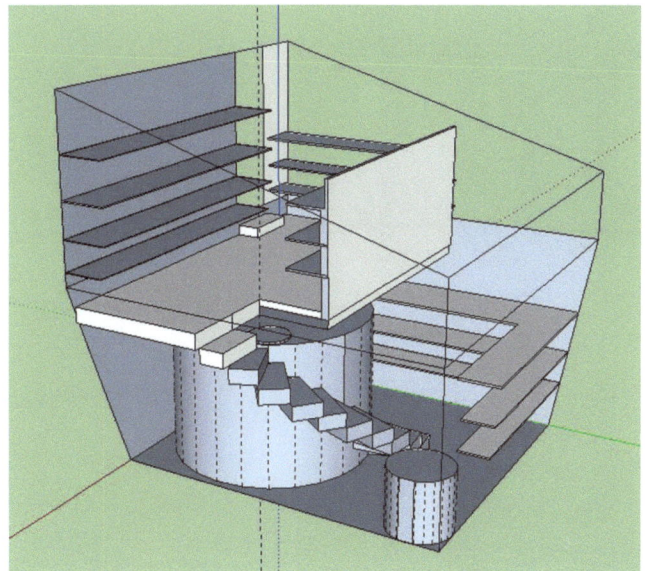

ing staircase would circle around the tank, and go down to the lower floor level, with more storage. By making an accurately scaled drawing I could visualize just how to do this and make it practical in terms of head room and such. I discovered that I needed to raise the north wall of the pantry about one extra foot for sufficient head room.

For optimal cool storage this would have been completely buried, but we wanted to be able to walk directly into it from the floor of the garage and it seemed easiest to just frame the roof and insulate it well. This meant that the side walls above grade would also need to be well insulated. For these walls we decided to try cordwood masonry construction.

Cordwood naturally provides good insulation because   the walls are thick (15 inches in this case) and

they have an open hollow core. You can see how that core was filled with a mixture of sawdust and lime to improve the insulation and make it unattractive to insects or mildew.

I was able to obtain all of the necessary cordwood very inexpensively with a firewood permit from local Forest Service land. Lightweight, softwood species are preferred for cordwood masonry, so these walls were made with aspen, cottonwood, and fir.

To provide some natural light in the pantry I used glass blocks in the cordwood wall as shown below.

The ceiling of the space was insulated with EPS panels cut to fit snugly between the roof supports, using two layers with an air space between them. Eventually I added a radiant barrier bubble wrap type of insulation to this mix for increased effectiveness. All of this insulation plus the enormous thermal mass of stored water and the fact that most of the pantry is buried in the ground keeps it from freezing in there, even in the high mountains of Colorado.

Many house designs would not easily accommodate a buried pantry, so another strategy for keeping a room cool is to locate it on the north side of the house, and have substantial air vents that are opened only at night during the warmer seasons. This requires a little more attention to maintain a cool temperature, but makes it possible to retrofit an existing house with a nice cool pantry. The room should be well insulated to keep it from warming up too much during the day.

The idea of having a large cool storage room makes so much sense to me that I think all houses should be designed this way. This facility uses no energy to keep things cool and promotes a lifestyle of fewer miles driven, along with a feeling of abundance and security. What a winning combination!

Sharing Facilities

Single family residential patterns are deeply ingrained in our culture. This chapter is about seeking ways to share our living experience with others.

Why should we do that? Because it is often the most ecological choice. Sharing facilities means that it is not necessary to have duplicate functions. For instance a group of people can share laundry facilities, kitchens, vehicles, guest quarters, meeting spaces, gardens, child care, libraries, and much more. This can have economic benefit as well as ecological benefit, not to mention the social value of interacting with like minded folks.

One common form of this sort of sharing is co-housing, where each family may have its own private living quarters, but many other functions are in common. Eco-villages are another expression of this impulse, and communes can be organized this way.

Rosana and I tried a kind of family communal experience when we bought Sunshine Camp with two of my sisters and their families and we all lived there together for nearly seven years. In many ways this former Catholic children's summer camp, situated not far from the Russian River in Northern California, was ideal for us.

There were already many existing buildings that could serve a variety of functions, including the row of cabins mentioned earlier that comprised Rosana and my house. In addition to these, there was the original farmhouse that had been there since before the camp was established, a caretaker's cottage, and other domestic cabins. Plus there was a store room, a kitchen and mess hall, a covered outdoor dining area with a fireplace, a walk-in cooler, toilet and shower facilities, and a chapel!

I designed the cartoon like sign over the entrance that signified three families coming together to enjoy a sunny life together. Pictured at the left of the entrance in the photo below is the bus home that we arrived in and a small cabin that we used for guests.

My older sister and her family inhabited the old farmhouse; her family was the largest and thus could utilize that larger house more effectively. This home can be seen near the center of the above photo. The main entrance to Sunshine Camp led directly to a large central courtyard around which most of the other buildings were arranged.

My younger sister and her family occupied this caretaker's cottage. It had its own kitchen and living room, as well as a sleeping loft. The adjacent store room also became part of their domain.

Both of my sisters were fiber artists, along with other talents, and we all shared a large studio with a floor to ceiling tapestry loom and a corner nook for my sheepskin slipper manufacturing business.

Another communal space that we all enjoyed was the little chapel. We kept it as entirely open space that was conducive to spiritual practice, tai chi classes, music events and parties.

In many ways it was the nicest space at Sunshine Camp, with a lovely natural pine wood interior and stained glass. I set up the piano that had been in my old bus in the chapel as well; that is what is visible near the center of the photo below.

My older sister was lounging in the sun while sorting out some hand died yarns for a tapestry project. Sharing that studio is a perfect example of the many benefits that can accrue through pooling resources in a communal setting.

This is a portrait of our entire family at that time. Rosana and I are at the far right of the photo. My older sister is standing at the center with her arm around her eldest child, and my younger sister is sitting next to her husband, with their child on her lap. Those were generally happy days for all of us.

delicious stuff. Rather than trying to can it we would freeze most of it in a huge freezer that was part of the walk-in cooler. Above, I was decanting some of that juice into a larger container. The hydraulic press itself can be seen behind me.

We experimented with sharing some garden space and I was tending one version of that. We also shared a flock of chickens. It was nice to be able to leave home on vacations or other trips and know that these things would be taken care of by other members of our extended family.

About half of the land that we acquired with Sunshine Camp was a mature apple orchard that we also cared for. We would often have prodigious harvests of Gravenstien apples that were excellent for juicing, so one of my brothers-in-law built a hefty juice pressing machine and we made many gallons of this

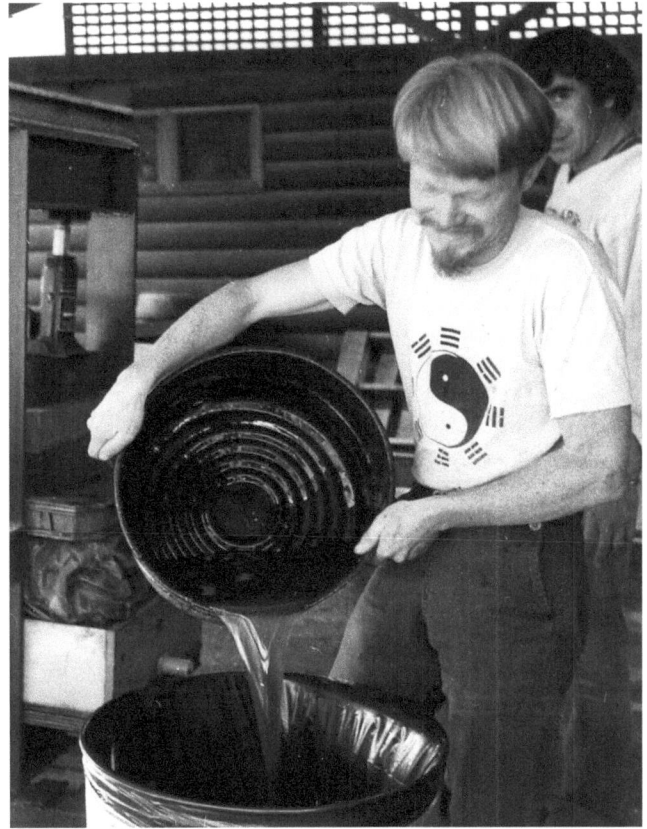

Another luxurious fruiting tree we enjoyed was a gigantic persimmon tree. These bright orange fruits would hang suspended on the leafless branches in the

51

late fall when we would gather to harvest them with a stretched sheet beneath the tree. We would eat some of them, but we sold most to an organic market in San Francisco, making more money with this single tree than with the entire apple orchard.

The center of much activity at Sunshine Camp was the community sand box. It was a magnet for all the kids, and this was both a blessing and a curse. They all had a great time playing there, but often we would be interrupted by screams of juvenile outrage as well. The sand box was located near the middle of the courtyard, so no one was immune from hearing this.

Another communal benefit was the shared use of an old red pickup truck that can be seen above, parked next to the weaving studio. The walk-in cooler has the Mobile Gas sign on its wall. There was a pear tree standing at the corner of the cooler.

The old kitchen became our canning and dying kitchen, and the old mess hall became our communal shop and laundry facility. The covered barbeque spot was

our periodic gathering place for communal meals. Mutual child care was a frequent occurrence.

Finances related to our mutual interests were coordinated so that one person was responsible for making sure that the mortgage, taxes, utilities, etc. were paid on time. We had a rudimentary system of shares according to the number of people in each family unit that determined how much money each family contributed to the communal pot. We also had some rent from tenants (often these were weaving apprentices,)

Over time, some of our communal habits changed; for instance, at first we tried eating most of our evening meals together, but that soon evolved into eating together less frequently. We occasionally had family meetings to discuss various issues, but these were not organized on any kind of a regular basis. I think that starting out as a close-knit family helped us maintain a sense of commitment and connection in a natural way.

We all treasure those days of living together at Sunshine Camp. The kids loved having such access to each other, and when my daughter was visiting, as she was when the photo of painted faces was taken, she had an extended family to connect with.

Of course, life has a way of evolving in unpredictable ways; family dynamics change, interests change, circumstances change. After about five years our commune began to fragment. My younger sister's partner wanted to start his own winery on his own property, and their relationship became strained. They needed to access their equity in the property, so my other sister and her husband and Rosana and I refinanced Sunshine Camp in order to buy them out.

Not long after that, my older sister and her husband's relationship loosened its bonding, and they also needed to access their equity in the property to evolve separate lives. At this point we knew that it was time to sell Sunshine Camp for all of us to move on toward new life goals. Rosana and I were feeling an urge to have control of our own future, unencumbered by communal choices as well.

So we did sell the property in the end. All of us prospered in many ways from the experience. Owning Sunshine Camp in common ultimately allowed each family to strike out independently and purchase other property as circumstances changed. And while we were living together we created even deeper bonds as a family.

Looking to the Future

The future is never known, but one can see the vectors that point in that direction. It seems to me that we are facing some real challenges as the Twentieth Century marches forward. The depletion of fossil fuel and other natural resources, climate change, population growth, economic inequality, and our reluctance to consciously face these problems will all severely impact lives in the future.

As individuals, all of this can seem overwhelming and beyond our control or influence. But ultimately it is only through individual action that we will address most of the challenges facing us. And this is where the topic of this book comes to the fore. Green remodeling is definitely a step in the right direction.

Conservation of energy through better insulation, the use of more efficient appliances, the introduction of renewable energy into the household, choosing compact or cooperative living arrangements, and employing building materials with low embodied energy can add up to great savings in energy consumption. And this helps with the economic part of the equation, as well as helps diminish the greenhouse gases that are driving climate change.

Wherever I am living, I am constantly taking stock of local building materials that can easily be utilized for projects. So when I want to build something, I run through my mental inventory of supplies and focus on those that best serve my needs. Often this results in recycling materials that would otherwise lie in a waste heap. Doing this not only makes me feel good, but it also saves a lot of money. Being resourceful is obviously a green trait.

Here is an example of what I mean about being resourceful: As I write this we are visiting some bare land that we own in Southern New Mexico. We are exploring ways that we might develop it some day. The soil on our property is almost perfect adobe soil, about 25% clay and 75% sand, so here is a free resource right under our feet, good for making adobe blocks, cob, rammed earth, or earthbag construction. There are also abundant stones on our property that could easily be used for many construction projects.

If I were to build a house in this climate, how would I design it? Well I know that in general the underground temperature is a fairly constant 65 degrees F., despite the annual range of well below freezing up to 115 degrees F. This makes me think that an underground house would be the way to go, since the gap between 65 degrees and a comfortable 72 degrees could easily be bridged with a small amount of passive solar heat. Summer air conditioning would be unnecessary. It would be easy to design a zero energy home in this climate!

If I were to create such an energy independent home I would be contributing to a sustainable future. If it were well built and durable it could provide inexpensive housing well beyond my lifetime. Many components of such a house could be recycled; in fact the entire house could be fashioned out of an existing steel vaulted structure (like a quonset) that was dismantled and reassembled underground on my property, so in a sense this could be considered a remodeling project.

And so my mind continues to explore possible futures, always wondering how best to utilize existing resources to make our future more pleasant.

Resources

My Websites:

www.greenhomebuilding.com was established in 2001 as a place to find comprehensive information about all aspects of sustainable architecture and natural building.

www.dreamgreenhomes.com features green plans for sale created by 18 architects and designers.

www.earthbagbuilding.com focuses on all aspects of building with earthbags.

www.naturalbuildingblog.com is a blog I share with Dr. Owen Geiger and is an eclectic mix of posts about sustainable living.

My DVD's:

A Sampler of Alternative Homes: Approaching Sustainable Architecture provides an overview of sustainable building concepts.

Building with Bags: How We Made Our Experimental Earthbag/Papercrete House chronicles three years of building a unique domed home.

Books:

Home Remodeling: Planning, Design, Construction by Fine Homebuilding, 2012.

Not So Big Remodeling: Tailoring Your Home for the Way You Really Live by Sarah Susanka and Marc Vassallo, 2012.

Making Better Buildings: A Comparative Guide to Sustainable Construction for Homeowners and Contractors by Chris Magwood, 2014.

Building on our past by Peter Hancock, 2011.

Green Home Improvement: 65 Projects That Will Cut Utility Bills, Protect Your Health & Help the the Environment by Daniel D. Chiras, 2008.

Tiny Homes, Simple Shelter: Scaling Back in the 21st Century by Lloyd Kahn, 2012.

Tiny House Design & Construction Guide by Dan Louche, 2012.

Passive Solar Architecture: Heating, Cooling, Ventilation, Daylighting and More Using Natural Flows by David Bainbridge and Ken Haggard, 2011.

Solar Home Heating Basics: A Green Energy Guide by Dan Chiras, 2012.

Heating or Cooling Your Building Naturally: Solar Architectural Solutions by Virginia B. Macdonald, 2006.

The Greened House Effect: Renovating Your Home with a Deep Energy Retrofit, by Jeff Wilson, 2013.

Power With Nature: Renewable Energy Options for Homeowners by Rex A. Ewing, 2012.

The Homeowner's Guide to Renewable Energy: Achieving Energy Independence through Solar, Wind, Biomass and Hydropower by Dan Chiras, 2006.

Design for Water: Rainwater Harvesting, Stormwater Catchment, and Alternate Water Reuse by Heather Kinkade-Levario, 2007.

compost toilets: a practical DIY guide by Dave Darby, 2012.

Back To Basics Complete Guide To Water Storage "How to Use Gray Water Tanks & Other Water Storage for Household & Emergency Use" by Julie Fryer, 2012.

Green Design: A Healthy Home Handbook by Alan Berman, 2008.

Green Your Home: The Complete Guide to Making Your New or Existing Home Environmentally Healthy by Jeanne Roberts, 2008.

Housing Reclaimed: Sustainable Homes for Next to Nothing by Jessica Kellner, 2011.

Natural Remodeling for the Not-So-Green House: Bringing Your Home into Harmony with Nature by Carol Venolia , Kelly Lerner, 2006.

The Complete Root Cellar Book: Building Plans, Uses and 100 Recipes by Maxwell and MacKenzie, 2010.